NIL NIL

Don Paterson was born in Dundee, Scotland, in 1963. He left school at sixteen, and since then has worked as a musician, moving to London in 1984. He won an Eric Gregory Award in 1990, and now lives in Brighton.

Nil Nil   DON PATERSON

faber and faber

LONDON · BOSTON

First published in 1993
by Faber and Faber Limited
3 Queen Square London WC1N 3AU

Photoset by Wilmaset Ltd, Wirral
Printed in England by Cox & Wyman Ltd, Reading, Berkshire

Don Paterson is hereby identified as author of this work in accordance
with Section 77 of the Copyright, Designs and Patents Act 1988

Two hundred cased bound copies of this first edition
have been produced exclusively
for members of the Poetry Book Society,
10 Barley Mow Passage, London W4

A CIP record for this book
is available from the British Library

ISBN 0 571 16808 6 (pbk)
     0 571 17087 0 (cased)

Thanks are due to the editors of the following, where some of these poems
first appeared:
*Bête Noire, The Gregory Poems, The Observer, Of Eros and Dust, The
Poetry Book Society Anthology, Poetry Review, Poetry Durham, The
Printer's Devil, The Rialto* and *Verse.*
The author gratefully acknowledges the financial assistance of the Society
of Authors.

10 9 8 7 6 5 4 3 2 1

For my mother and father

Contents

The Ferryman's Arms, 1
Morning Prayer, 2
Filter, 3
Exeunt:
   (i) Drop Serene, 4
  (ii) Curtains, 4
  (iii) Bird, 5
  (iv) The Electric Brae, 5
Heliographer, 7
Sunset, Visingsö, 8
Ezekiel, 9
Sisters, 11
Obeah, 12
Orchitis, 13
Close, 15
Seed, 17
Mooncalf, 18
An Elliptical Stylus, 20
Amnesia, 22
Heredity, 24
The Alexandrian Library, 25
Next to Nothing, 34
The Trans-Siberian Express, 35
Pioneer, 36
Shhh, 37
Restitution, 38
The Clearing House, 39
Wind-Tunnel, 40
Poem (after Skala), 41
Fraud, 42
Dinosaurs, 44
Dirty Weekend, 45
Graffito, 46

Perigee, 47
Bedfellows, 48
Countdown, 49
Beltane, 50
Nil Nil, 51

Slamming Door:
  A real door slammed off-stage gives the best effect.

Michael Green, *Stage Noises And Effects*

The Ferryman's Arms

About to sit down with my half-pint of Guinness
I was magnetized by a remote phosphorescence
and drawn, like a moth, to the darkened back room
where a pool-table hummed to itself in the corner.
With ten minutes to kill and the whole place deserted
I took myself on for the hell of it. Slotting
a coin in the tongue, I looked round for a cue –
while I stood with my back turned, the balls were deposited
with an abrupt intestinal rumble; a striplight
batted awake in its dusty green cowl.
When I set down the cue-ball inside the parched D
it clacked on the slate; the nap was so threadbare
I could screw back the globe, given somewhere to stand –
as physics itself becomes something negotiable
a rash of small miracles covers the shortfall:
I went on to make an immaculate clearance.
A low punch with a wee dab of side, and the black
did the vanishing trick while the white stopped
before gently rolling back as if nothing had happened,
shouldering its way through the unpotted colours.

The boat chugged up to the little stone jetty
without breaking the skin of the water, stretching,
as black as my stout, from somewhere unspeakable
to here, where the foaming lip mussitates endlessly,
trying, with a nutter's persistence, to read
and re-read the shoreline. I got aboard early,
remembering the ferry would leave on the hour
even for only my losing opponent;
but I left him there, stuck in his tent of light, sullenly
knocking the balls in, for practice, for next time.

Morning Prayer
(*after Rimbaud*)

I spend my life sitting, like an angel at the barber's,
with a mug in one hand, fag in the other,
my froth-slabbered face in the gantry mirror
while the smoke towels me down, warm and white.

On the midden of desire, the old dreams
still hold their heat, ferment, gently ignite –
once, my heart had thrown its weight behind them
but it saps itself now, stews in its own juice.

Having stomached my thoughts like a horrible linctus
– swilled down with, oh, fifteen, twenty pints –
I am roused only by the most bitter necessities:

then, the air high with the smell of opened cedar,
I pish gloriously into the dawn skies
while below me the spattered ferns nod their assent.

Filter

Thrown out in a glittering arc
   as clear as the winterbourne,
the jug of Murphy's I threw back
   goes hissing off the stone.

Whatever I do with all the black
   is my business alone.

Exeunt

(i)

DROP SERENE

He poured the warm, clear guck into the mould
in which he'd already composed, with tweezers,
dead wasps on an everlasting flower
or ants filing over a leaf. When it was cold
he slaved at the surface, softening the camber
till it sat with the row of blebs on his mantelpiece,
each with its sequestered populace
like a hiccup in history, scooped out of amber.

As if it might stall the invisible cursor
drawing a blind down each page of his almanac
or the blank wall of water that always kept pace,
glittering an inch, half an inch from his back.
He was out in the garden, digging the borders
when it caught him, in a naturalistic pose.

(ii)

CURTAINS

You stop at the tourist office in Aubeterre,
a columbarium of files and dockets.
She explains, while you flip through the little leaflets
about the chapel and the puppet-theatre,
that everything is boarded up till spring,
including – before you can ask – the only hotel.
A moped purrs through the unbroken drizzle.
You catch yourself checking her hands for rings.

She prepares a light supper; you chat,
her fussy diction placing words in air
like ice in water. She leads you to her room
but gets the shivers while you strip her bare;
lifting her head, you watch her pupils bloom
into the whole blue iris, then the white.

(iii)

BIRD

The wind baffled lightly as they filled the grave
and a queasy flutter left us, the last faint
ripple of the peristaltic wave
that ushered her out. In eight months, her complaint
had whittled her down to the palsied sylph
who filched the car-keys from her snoring spouse
and went out to prove a point; then found herself,
like Alice, on the wrong side of the glass.

Later, back at the house, I overheard
the disembodied voices in the hall
where George, who'd only last another year,
was trying to be philosophical:
*Ach, there was nothin' o' her. She was nae mair
than a sparra, nae mair than a wee bird.*

(iv)

THE ELECTRIC BRAE

For three days and three nights, he has listened
to the pounding of a terrible jug band
now reduced to a wheezy concertina
and the disinterested thump of a tea-chest bass.
It seems safe to look: wires trail on the pillowcase,
a drip swings overhead; then the clear tent

becomes his father's clapped-out Morris Minor,
rattling towards home. The windscreen presents
the unshattered myth of a Scottish spring;
with discreet complicity, the road
swerves to avoid the solitary cloud.
On an easy slope, his father lets the engine
cough into silence. Everything is still.
He frees the brake: the car surges uphill.

Heliographer

I thought we were sitting in the sky.
My father decoded the world beneath:
our tenement, the rival football grounds,
the long bridges, slung out across the river.
Then I gave myself a fright
with the lemonade bottle. Clunk —
the glass thread butting my teeth
as I bolted my mouth to the lip.

Naw . . . copy me. It's how the grown-ups drink.
Propped in my shaky,
single-handed grip,
I tilted the bottle towards the sun
until it detonated with light,
my lips pursed like a trumpeter's.

Sunset, Visingsö
(*after Jørn-Erik Berglund*)

The lake has simplified
to one sleep-wave
bounced between shores.

All evening,
as superstition requires,
my eyes have not left it –

the fabulous animal
I will flay for the colour
its skin grows when it dreams.

Ezekiel

(i)

He was struggling down the ladder between decks,
his free arm lightly cradling the compass
like a great egg; he was sure he felt a pluck
at his chest, swaying above the last rung.
Imagining the ship about to rock
he leant to compensate: the compass stung
like a mule. They found him there, unconscious,
the gyro beside him, purring in its box.

The men from the university assemble
in a toolshed on a bleak Dundee estate
politely clearing their throats while he unveils
the squat and massive tree of gyroscopes
and builds a rough chord on it, till the rumble
focuses to a pure hum. The coughing stops:
he has unlocked the hammer within the anvil.
It drills on his workbench, begins to levitate.

(ii)

The news of our approach had crossed the nation
entirely, so it seemed, by word of mouth –
a vast network, so sensitively primed
that by the time we rolled up in the hired Toyota
the three Professors of Music from Oxford University
had long secured their place in local myth.
Eager to help us with our dissertation
they had already booked the venue, fixed the time.

All time is lost in the music, and the drained jug.
When it returns, it catches at us like a ripcord –
the skipped beat from reel to jig –
instantaneously, the ring of dancers blur,
resolving as a wheel within a wheel,
a flashing zoetrope, rims full of eyes . . .
At the point the tune turns back to bite its tail
they pause, then stamp the floor from under us.

Sisters
(*for Eva*)

Back then, our well of tenements
powered the black torch that could find
the moon at midday: four hours later
the stars would be squandered on us.

     *

As the sun spread on her freckled back
I felt as if I'd turned the corner
to a bright street, scattered with coins;
for weeks, I counted them over and over.

     *

In a dark kitchen, my ears still burning,
I'd dump the lilo, binoculars, almanac
and close the door on the flourishing mess
of Arabic and broken lines.

     *

Though she swears they're not identical
when I dropped her sister at the airport
my palms hurt as she spoke my name
and I bit my tongue back when I kissed her.

     *

Nowadays, having shrunk the sky
to a skull-sized planetarium
— all fairy-lights and yawning voice-overs —
I only stay up for novae, or comets.

     *

Some mornings I wake, and fantasize
I've slipped into her husband's place
as he breathes at her back, sliding his tongue
through Fomalhaut and the Southern Cross.

[11]

Obeah

My life became one long apostrophe —
muttering the three ur-syllables of her name,
doodling her initials to a cryptogram.
Chain-smoking and the 'slavery of tea and coffee'
left me light enough to forge her succubus
tooth by tooth, the tiny hands and feet,
the calves like folded wings . . . On one such night
I got up and hit out west, passing her house;

bumped up on the kerb, cars sat in line
like after-hour drinkers elbowed at the bar,
hushed as the stranger walks in off the moor —
their premonitory stare, blank as a mirror.
I saw the dawn scried in each polished screen,
the gibbeted mascots as I drew in closer.

Orchitis

(i)

My Irish cousin knew all about the ailment.
Terrified, I held the line while he fished through
his lecture notes: he had the word for it.
(Conversely, hers had been a bloodless coup –
our little arriviste, only just present
as her pulse's imperceptible backbeat.)

I hung up, and rolled onto my left side.
The Lambeg's feverish and bolstered thud
conducted me through sleep's unlisted backstreets
where my cousin works in grubby whites, dismembering
something at needlepoint. Under my sheets
I weigh his blades against the ticking membrane.

(ii)

While he staked out my back with his long pins
I fixed upon my lifeless effigy –
faithfully reproduced, its tiny limbs
bent in stylized attitudes of agony.
He rotated each needle in turn, touching my wrist
for the lightened ictus, the shift of emphasis.

The day after, I joined the others on our sally
to study Irish music, with the blessing
of Mr Art C. Grant of Piccadilly;
like most blow-ins, our coy itinerary
never within a hundred miles of crossing
the dotted line, marked out for surgery.

(iii)

With recent developments, the biggest problem
has been the insensitive use of modern percussion
tending, as it does, to overstate
the accentual 'lift', integral to the tradition.
Even the humble goatskin-headed frame-drum
(which, prior to 1950, was only played

on St Stephen's Day – the seasonal leitmotif
in the hunting of the sacrificial wren)
has been regarded as a growing menace;
questioned on the matter, Seamus Ennis
remarked that the best way to play the bodhran
was with a knife.

Close

She was two months late.
Our tiny ghost
ignored the threats
and blithely crossed

her final deadline,
the sincerity
of its ambition
embarrassing me.

As we stood in file
at the taxi-rank
beside the pool
we watched some drunk

practically choke
trying to demonstrate
the butterfly stroke
to his drunken mate.

Bowing, the swimmer
left his audience
with the prefatory shimmer
of the dream sequence

as briefly, water
rewrote the lines,
shuffling the letters
of the High Street signs.

Too weak to stand,
the muggy night
slumped to the ground
while we both fought

for breathing space:
the acrid drizzle
stung my face
like pins and needles.

Seed

Parenthood is no more than murder
by degrees, the classic martyr-
dom. All the old myths are true: I pushed him under,
scything his bollocks off, stealing his thunder.

Leaking cock or bodged withdrawal,
ruptured condom; month-long vigil —
it is I who just escape with my life.
My child is hunting me down like a thief.

Mooncalf

He remembered that dog – more beloved
than any child, her own unaided work –
and the afternoon he'd spent watching her wank,
following her fingertips' slow levigation;
how the light was gently drawn into the livid,
tightening circle of her concentration
before a black nose snuffled out, and he slid
away from her - black-eyed, sleek as a seal.

Then he pictured her behind the wheel,
driving to the vet's. The sky had cleared;
just a few planes needling the ionosphere,
their contrails unfurling into the weird cirrus –
crabbed, dead galaxies, or tattered veils
like egg-white in water. *It won't be serious.*
He parted the shaking fur – there; he could feel
the soft nub, sickeningly off-centre.

He'd found his brother sunning on the counter,
posed with the green plums; the stillborn's sealing-wax
dubbed on his little, epicene hunchback
aping their white-lead bloom, the casual slit
of their spines: just one long tacking-stitch, snuck under
to a bald cloaca, where the stalk curled out
like fish-stool. They all held by their own winter,
picked too early, frozen at the core.

And so he died, in the bathtub of his bachelor
slum, watching the spat of grey jism
congeal before him, twitching like ectoplasm
as it knitted itself into shreds of tissue
and bobbed towards the blinding white shore
in a bluestone sea, his God-given, perfect issue.
The thing began to bleat, and soared
from the dirty bathwater, like the sun.

An Elliptical Stylus

My uncle was beaming: 'Aye, yer elliptical stylus –
fairly brings out a' the wee details.'
Balanced at a fraction of an ounce
the fat cartridge sank down like a feather;
music billowed into three dimensions
as if we could have walked between the players.

My Dad, who could appreciate the difference,
went to Largs to buy an elliptical stylus
for our ancient, beat-up Phillips turntable.
We had the guy in stitches: 'You can't . . .
er . . . you'll have to *upgrade your equipment*.'
Still smirking, he sent us from the shop
with a box of needles, thick as carpet-tacks,
the only sort they made to fit our model.

(Supposing I'd been *his* son: let's eavesdrop
on 'Fidelities', the poem I'm writing now:
*The day my father died, he showed me how
he'd prime the deck for optimum performance:
it's that lesson I recall – how he'd refine
the arm's weight, to leave the stylus balanced
somewhere between ellipsis and precision,
as I gently lower the sharp nip to the line
and wait for it to pick up the vibration
till it moves across the page, like a cardiograph . . .*)

We drove back slowly, as if we had a puncture;
my Dad trying not to blink, and that man's laugh
stuck in my head, which is where the story sticks,
and any attempt to cauterize this fable
with something axiomatic on the nature
of articulacy and inheritance,
since he can well afford to make his *own*
excuses, you your own interpretation.
But if you still insist on resonance —
I'd swing for him, and every other cunt
happy to let my father know his station,
which probably includes yourself. To be blunt.

Amnesia

I was, as they later confirmed, a very sick boy.
The star performer at the meeting-house,
my eyes rolled back to show the whites, my arms
outstretched in catatonic supplication
while I gibbered impeccably in the gorgeous tongues
of the aerial orders. On Tuesday nights, before
I hit the Mission, I'd nurse my little secret:
Blind Annie Spall, the dead evangelist
I'd found still dying in creditable squalor
above the fishmonger's in Rankine Street.
The room was ripe with gurry and old sweat;
from her socket in the greasy mattress, Annie
belted through hoarse chorus after chorus
while I prayed loudly, absently enlarging
the crater that I'd gouged in the soft plaster.
Her eyes had been put out before the war,
just in time to never see the daughter
with the hare-lip and the kilt of dirty dishtowels
who ran the brothel from the upstairs flat
and who'd chap to let me know my time was up,
then lead me down the dark hall, its zoo-smell,
her slippers peeling off the sticky lino.
At the door, I'd shush her quiet, pressing
my bus-fare earnestly into her hand.

Four years later. Picture me: drenched in patchouli,
strafed with hash-burns, casually arranged
on Susie's bed. Smouldering frangipani;
Dali's *The Persistence of Memory*;
pink silk loosely knotted round the lamp
to soften the light; a sheaf of Penguin Classics,
their spines all carefully broken in the middle;
a John Martyn album mumbling through the speakers.
One hand was jacked up her skirt, the other trailing
over the cool wall behind the headboard
where I found the hole in the plaster again.
The room stopped like a lift; Sue went on talking.
It was a nightmare, Don. We had to gut the place.

Heredity

Our great progenitor, still in his dog-collar,
is the only innocent here, unabashed
as he splays the tines on his Hitler moustache
till it fits painlessly. When challenged, others declare
a horse with no head, a clipper with webbed sails,
a bearskinned sentry, fused to his post.
A belated crack – the fangs of Dracula fall
to the man they say I now resemble most.

At some point, I have looked like all of them –
now typecast, mortgaged to the hilt, they harbour
the pain encoded in the creaks and murmurs
still visited upon each new conception,
passing between us like a whispering game,
a matter of personal interpretation.

My maiden aunt fusses from seat to seat
quietly establishing just who
wants peas or carrots, boiled or roast potatoes,
which of us favour the dark meat.

The Alexandrian Library

Nothing is ever lost; things only become irretrievable.
What is lost, then, is the method of their retrieval, and
what we rediscover is not the thing itself, but the
overgrown path, the secret staircase, the ancient sewer.

François Aussemain, *Pensées*

The lights go up: you find yourself facing
the wrangle of metal outside the Great Terminus.
You are poised on the end of the platform, the word
on the tip of its tongue: *There!* you shout, spotting
two rails still in spasm; they flex and unflex
like the last eels alive in the bucket.

As the train slithers out, you hang from the guard's van
to watch the tracks flailing from under the wheels;
this is no silver clew you will pay out behind you.
A few landmarks sail past in the wrong permutation
before the train pulls the ground over its head
and goes rocketing into the dark.

The intricate snare-rolls converge to beat
a slow tattoo as you file past the stations
sealed up between wars, like family vaults;
though you make out the posters for Eye Salts and Bloater Paste
the nameplates have all been unscrewed from the walls,
but peeling the gaffa-tape back from the map
you uncover the names of decanonized saints
and football clubs, now long-extinct.
Hours later, the train slams into the open –
light booms through the carriage; the sky is so low
you instinctively duck. After a rough night
the sun thuds away in its bleary corona;
a slack river drags itself under the hills

where the sheep swarm like maggots. These were the
                                        battlegrounds
abandoned in laughter, the borders no more
than feebly disputed; a land with no history,
there being no victors to write it. You lean
from the window to use the last shot in the spool:
the print slinks out like a diseased tongue.
When the laminates clear, the margin of black
has already begun to encroach from the left.
You pass the closed theme-park, a blighted nine-holer,
the stadium built for a cancelled event
now host to less fair competition:
a smatter of gunfire pinks at your cheek
as it leans on the glass. Now the line curves
over pitheads and slagheaps, long towns with one street
where only the kirk strains much above ground-level.
A station draws up, and slots into place
to fill the whole train with its name: COWDENBEATH

You alight; then a sharp suck of air at your back
whips you round – no train, no tracks, no ballast . . .
only the sleepers are left undisturbed
and bed themselves into the weeds. You jump down
and walk to the end of the line, where the sleepers
go angling into the ground, one by one;
it takes twice as long to walk back, since you stand
on the disinterred arc of a gigantic millwheel,
a cog in the planet's own secret machinery.
When you finally catch up with the platform, no one
is waiting to tear up the ticket you've lost
and the buses are off, so you set out on foot
for the northernmost tip of a council estate,
the last Pictish enclave, where beaky degenerates
silently moon at the back of the shops
while girls with disastrous make-up and ringworm
stalk past with their heads down and arms folded,

You are drawn inside the stone mouth of a tenement
where a young woman, soaping it out on her knees,
watches you try the blue door by the bin-recess
before shaking her head, then nodding you over.
You walk on to the soft punch of alien cooking,
now confused, as she ushers you past the wrecked pay-phone,
the windowless box-room, the ghost of a door
in the partition-wall, and then into the kitchen
where the smell and the steam-driven clitter of pot-lids
sends you rushing out into the drying-green.
Before you, surrounded by twelve of the blue doors,
are thirteen allotments; you make for the one
claimed only by nettles and scrub, with few clues
to the previous owner (potsherds, an old purse, some rope?),
then tie up the fence-gate and sit down to think.

Think:
the brain,
having worked itself
into huge furrows through aeons
of failure to recollect something important,
still hoarding the nut of the pineal eye
where, neglected, the soul has reverted to grit;
though you frantically pass a charge over and over
the calcified circuitry, nothing will take
so you lower yourself down the chain of command
till you locate the flaw: the synaptic lacuna
where the spark of your most-treasured memory
finally fails in the crossing
and sinks in the gap
like Leander.

In
the dark
of your anorak pocket
your lily hand flutters awake:

three inches of card have slipped down from your cuff
like a hustler's ace. Exposed to the light
your lost ticket turns itself into a business card:
Harry Sturgis: Remaindered and Second-Hand Books.
On the back is a street-map, criss-crossed by two arrows;
one points to the shop, and one to a complicated
bit in the corner, bearing the legend:
You Are Here.

                   You are there, on the breast of MacPhailor
                                      Street,
in the Heart of the Land of the Beaverboard Curtains,
where the cassies are frying with drizzle.
About to turn back from the boarded-up address
you notice the gap in the palings, the steps,
and gingerly feed yourself into the basement
where a rain-sodden carton of slushy romances
has decomposed into one big one. You shove
at the unnumbered door; there is a short kerfuffle
as books topple over behind it.

Harry himself does not stir from the counter
where he humps his one huge eyebrow, plotting daggers
on the Spot the Ball comp. on the back of the *Herald*
(*Brechin v Raith, March 15th,*
Conditions: muddy. Attendance: 52).
A sign reads 'No Browsin – Dont Waist Your Time, Ask';
the walls are so stap-full, they look on the brink
of disgorging their contents, delivering up
the death you so often have dreamed of.
To your left is a corridor, book-clogged, low-ceilinged;
a cheesy light clings to the concatenation
of friable bell-wire and 40W bulbs.
You edge past the stuffed thing on guard at the entrance
while burnt stour and mildew make grabs for your throat.

This is no disappointment — each title bears witness
to Harry's appalling librarianship:
The Story of Purfling; *Living with Alzheimer's*;
Mastering the Nursery Cannon; back issues
of *Button Collector*, *Dogfighter Monthly*
and *Spunk*; *Mad Triste*; *The Use of Leucotomy
in the Treatment of Pre-Menstrual Stress*;
16 RPM — a Selective Discography;
Diabetic Desserts All the Family Will Love;
Origamian specials — *The Scissor Debate*;
Urine — The Water of Life; *The King's Gambit —
Play it to Win*; *The Al Bowlly Songbook*;
Beyond Dance — New Adventures in Labanotation;
The Volapük Scout Manual; piles of old sick-notes,
unmarked exam papers, staff memoranda
on Portion Control, and risible stabs
at the Unified Field Theory, furtively mimeoed
in the janitor's office in playtime;
The Late Correspondence of Breece D'J'Pancake
and *The Poems of Erich von Däniken*.

                        You have arrived,
in a fashion to which you have paid no attention,
at this small diverticulum, its wittering striplight
a gangrenous purple at either extremity.
On a whim, you lift a few books from the shelf —
I am John's Prostate; *The Cardinal's Mistress*;
the Book Club edition of *Josephine Mützenbacher*;
A Seven-Day Thinking Course; *You and Your Autoharp*
and *Steal This Book* (signed, some foxing of endpapers)
— exposing the layer below; this yields up
Stanyhurst's *Vergil* and Pye's *Analecta*
(uncut); *Lady Bumtickler's Revels*; the Bible
they quietly pulped when the proof-reader's shopping-list
turned up in Numbers, thanks to some dickhead
apprentice compositor. You wistfully leaf

through a spineless edition of poor Hartley Coleridge:
No hope have I to live a deathless name . . .

Squeering hard into the hole you have made
a new seam grows visible, packed like anthracite;
you work out a grimoire in horrible waxpaper,
a lost Eddic cycle of febrile monotony,
Leechdom and Wortcunning; *Living with Alzheimer's*
and Tatwine's gigantic *Aenigmae Perarduae*,
the whole thing a triple acrostic, and scrawled
onto wine-splattered oak-tag in the infantile hand
of the biggest joke in the scriptorium.

A tongue of dust, tasting of naphtha and pollen,
creeps out from the little vault, licking your hand
as it swims to the back and starts faking around;
from the scrips and the ashes you manage to fish out
a short monograph on the storage of turnips,
two bloodstained scytalae (wound round your arm
they read something about reinforcements); the Gospel
According to Someone Who Once Shagged the Sister
of St James the Less; Chaldean star charts
mistaken for blotter, glutted with star-showers
and fat supernovae; The Lost Book of Jasher,
who could barely predict his own lunchtime.
Lastly, two scrolls trundle out to present themselves;
the name on the tag leaves you gasping for air:

Φρυνιχος

     Divine Phrynicus, Lost Lord of Lost Hope,
of whom almost nothing survives but reports
of his greatness; Phrynicus, whose plays stuffed *Medea*
into third place in the Tragedy Contests,
one of them leaving the crowd so distressed
the authorities punished the man for his hubris.

But as you read on, your jaw falls even further
as you learn the real reason they fined him . . .
Mercifully, only the first act of *Battus*,
though *Myndon*, in all its woeful entirety,
unfurls to the floor with no flourish of trumpets
but a strangled toot, forlorn and wanky
like something some arsehole might blow in your face
at the end of a terrible party.

Wearily, you bury your arm to the shoulder,
your fingers at last touching stone; but your fingertips
go scuttling blindly across the clay prisms,
tracing the fugitive spoor of cuneiform
while you helplessly mouth the grim stories it tells,
the vowels shifting back down your throat as the language
grows cruder and cruder, turning the air blue.
Now, in the ur-bark your voice has become,
reputations deflate, heroes dwindle, till finally
with Helen revealed as a fifteen-stone catamite,
the Epic of Gilgamesh edited down
to the original camping-weekend, and *Yahweh*
just the noise that they made when the chisel slipped,
you swallow your tongue, and gag on the silence.
Your fingers rest on a great brass ring,
blissfully free from inscription; you stroke it
for comfort, and draw its dull glint through the dark,
so soothed by its light it takes seconds to register
the huge head on the end of it.

When your brain catches up with your legs, the damage
is already done, and every new turning
only compounds the original error;
slowing down to think, you only bring closer
the stamping and snorting behind you.
(How many times in the past has this horror
sent down, or sent up from the Dream below Dreams,
turned up in the whorehouse, the hospital corridor,

the laundrette, the lift or the school-dinner queue
to ferret you out of the dream-warren?
How many times have you found yourself scrabbling
up through the fathoms of earth, to emerge
nose-first from the turndown, your heart like a fist
at the trap you have only just bolted behind you?
And remember: in this world, as well as the real one,
none of the real doors are marked with big arrows.)
Going into a skid on the blindest of corners
you trip on a pile of misprinted erratum slips
and fly into space: landing, your fall
is conveniently broken by the full print-run
of *Gems of the Muse*, Vol. 9 (Buckfast Books);
and rifling through the top copy, you find it –
there, in the third line of *What is Emotion?*
by *Linda* – a misplaced full stop starts to spin,
then expands, like a dead junkie's pupil, engulfing
the page, your hands, then your wrists, arms and torso,
the beast at your back, and the rest of it.

This is
Planck-Time
Absolute Zero
Albedo Fuck-All:
Luna Obscura, the old shunting-yard
where the dreams float to rest on their silent buffers.
Falling in with the zombified denizens (like them,
you imagine yourself quite alone) you begin
the nightly migration from Mare Incuborum
to Mare Insomniae, dustbowl to dustbowl,
ashpit to ashpit, your whole body polarized
by the rising meniscus, its cold incandescence
slitting your eyes with its light.

A sickle of moonlight
rests on the curve of her hip.
Through the net curtains, one night short of full,
the ancient bull-roarer hums low in the sky.
Your dearest one shifts in her sleep to lie facing you,
two tiny white moons in her wide-open eyes
and the wrong voice in her mouth:

So with one bound, Jack was free . . .
and he woke up to find it had all been a dream.
But when do you wake from the book of the dream,
shrug it off with a cold shower, a shot of black coffee?
There can be no forgetting; even after the fire
the archives are always somewhere intact —
in the world, or that part of the mind that the mind
cannot contemplate. But you have forgotten
the book you brought back; it lies on your pillow
as real as the pennies the tooth-fairies bring
or the horse's head left by the heavy squad.
Don't open it — the pages look blank in this light,
and tomorrow the words will draw your pen through them
until you have traced the whole terrible story
and think it your own. But no one man can own
a library book, and this library book
is already long overdue; hand it back —
there will be no tart letters or final demands,
just a knock at the door where no door ever was.

And you listen:
but it is only the milk-train

or your heart,
pounding over the points.

Next to Nothing

The platform clock stuck on the golden section:
ten to three. A frozen sun. The dead
acoustic of a small county; a dog-bark
is a short tear in the sky, above the wood.
The fixed stars crowd below the jagged awning.

Over the tracks, the ghost of the lame porter
stabs a brush along the ground, then vanishes.
The clock puts on a minute, tips the balance

and the stars fall as dust; birdsong thaws in the air.
The recorded voice addresses its own echo.

The Trans-Siberian Express
(for Eva)

One day we will make our perfect journey –
the great train smashing through Dundee, Brooklyn
and off into the endless tundra,
the earth flattening out before us.

I follow your continuous arrival,
shedding veil after veil after veil –
the automatic doors wincing away
while you stagger back from the buffet

slopping *Laphroaig* and decent coffee
until you face me from that long enfilade
of glass, stretched to vanishing point
like facing mirrors, a lifetime of days.

Pioneer

It's here I would have come to pass away
the final hour before the boat's departure;
the bluff side of the Law, between the harbour
and the dark, cetacean barrow of Balgay.

Twin trains of headlights inched across the river –
the homebound day-shift – trail-blazing cars
like angels on the starry escalator
of the bridge's tapering, foreshortened spar.

I tried to see it as a burning lance
angling for the slicked, black shoals of Fife
or a bowsprit, swung and steeved against the south

to help ride out her hellish afterlife:
the stubborn, rammish sap still on my hands,
the taste of her, like a coin laid in my mouth.

Shhh

Then, it was natural
to hear the sea remembered
in those stony airlocks and chambers
though I soon knew it might as well
be anything – forest fires, landslides, hurricanes
falsified by distance
or amplification; the white noise
of the wilder elements

or the mild chaos
as she puts her lips to your ear
and you cock your brain to catch
her general drift – the blandishments,
the breath drawn at your touch:
I no longer believe what I hear.

Restitution

The Book of Change, through all my feverish dealings,
produced the same response: *Li. Flaming Beauty*.
Her note came late, as if, to spare my feelings
the postman had snuck round with it, off-duty.
Before the last three pennies chattered down
the first few lines had made the outcome clear:
So great is the obstruction, the midday sun
appears as a tiny star.

I kept her letters, still cheap-scented, vital,
pressed the life from them between my books,
shook out the straws of sentimental detail,
laid half aside, discarded the remainder,
then cropped them to a line's length: they lie in stooks
as trim as yarrow stalks, as dry as tinder.

The Clearing House
(*for Gillian Brodie*)

The door opens on the right scene, like a bookmark.
Finding a thread, you lift it from my suit
in an act of continuity; but
four years of marriages and separations,
the virgin births and instantaneous deaths
restore, by increments, the proper distance.

Getting here, I took my old short cut,
leaving the road to walk across the park,
though I only made it halfway through; the footpath
ran on beneath a fence, into the dark.
I looked into the mess of open foundations,
half-built walls, little piles of earth.

Wind-Tunnel

Sometimes, in autumn, the doors between the days
fall open; in any other season
this would be a dangerous mediumship
though now there is just the small exchange of air
as from one room to another. A street
becomes a faint biography: you walk
through a breath of sweetpea, pipesmoke, an old perfume.

But one morning, the voices carry from everywhere:
from the first door and the last, two whistling draughts
zero in with such unholy dispatch
you do not scorch the sheets, or wake your wife.

Poem
(after Ladislav Skala)

The ship pitched in the rough sea
and I could bear it no longer
so I closed my eyes
and imagined myself on a ship
in a rough sea-crossing.

The woman rose up below me
and I could bear it no longer
so I closed my eyes
and imagined myself making love
to the very same woman.

When I came into the world
I closed my eyes
and imagined my own birth.
Still
I have not opened my eyes to this world.

Fraud

(i)

From the Kiev's ersatz cosmopolitan
(dusty bidets, loop-tape bossa nova)
I look down on my home town's doppelgänger –
not your clubbable, exchange-trip 'twin'
but the sort that stares back from the shaving-mirror
gap-toothed, yellow-eyed, malignant.
Crossing an empty square in Bratislava
I passed the brother that had died at birth,
his features warped by amateur dentistry.

'You can't take it with you!' admonishes Elva,
of whom I have grown too fond – this, despite
the worrying strabismus, snaggle-tooth.
I bite my lip throughout most of the flight
until the pilot, ending the suspense,
negotiates my mass back into weight;
a slow embodiment, like sitting in the bath
with the water draining out. As we touch land
my fingers loosen on the freezing coins.

(ii)

Reaching below the sink, I fumble
for the 5p slot; the padlocked meter
admits the bastard heraldry
of my last remaining 2Kcs piece
with a wink, and makes a small advance.
Submerged, apart from the face,
my body, with each insufflation,
displaces two lungfuls of water;
the overflow draws its commission.

As I baled myself out so incessantly
I had practically fallen asleep
when my heart cut out, from sheer indifference.
I leapt overboard – the white suds spattered
the floor like guano – then, winded, gawped
as though the penny'd finally dropped
to my own long-standing cuckoldry
or else I'd accidentally stumbled
on the test for adulterated gold.

Dinosaurs

(i)

Overweight, belligerent,
we share this tiny patch;
passing, we exchange a grunt,
a subcutaneous itch.

A hundred times we've had the chance
to leave, but stick together;
now there's a dead ache in my joints
like a terrible change in the weather.

(ii)

The nurse conducts the exercise
in limited extinction:
the plate prepared, the source exposed
with no more than a glib nictation.

I am told to get dressed and go home.
Later, in my absence
the doctors make their guesses from
the holes left by my bones.

Dirty Weekend

We hit the one-way, and are drawn in a spiral
towards the town centre and then down the plughole
of the Ascot Hotel. In an overpriced bedroom
we dry-rut and argue, then sink to bad dreams

where the day is re-screened; only something is odd –
the original cast has been shot, and replaced
by policemen, old lovers, dead relatives; God
in a good-humoured, masterly cameo, plays

Himself, strolling over the set, à la Hitchcock.
We wake to no birds, but the smell of the glassworks
which hangs like the ghost of a terrible sock
while we try out *Resolves, Askits, Answers*, like passwords.

Now skint, but still looking as though we had roughed it,
we circle, ignoring the signs, till we round on
the town's single exit, messily grafted
to the motorway, straightening its seam towards London.

Graffito

Her volte-face left him feeling idiotic, a
tourist with a map he couldn't read,
thumbing apart a bashful A–Z
after some retracted street – guilt-trip erotica,

the stuff that made him go weak at the knees:
the imperatives of sex and Calvinism
locked in an argument, original as sin
but still compelling – the backside's glorious schism
(its clenched resolve produced a teddy bear's grin)
presented in a pert, barefaced pricktease

while each dumb caress seared through him like sciatica.
Stuck for words, and idling in her bed
his ragged thumbnail scrawled an X in red
across her arse's silky-smooth hieratica.

Perigee

Freak alignments. I am the best man,
she, the bridesmaid. John, the resident MC,
once our playground quarry, does not complain
when we corner him, frisking for his master key.

Our affair was stripped of all the usual padding –
just a flat joke about not getting 'committed'
and a serviceable number by Joan Armatrading –
but we honed the *ruse de guerre* that first outwitted,
then destroyed our partners. I'd do sentry duty,
she, the dangerous stuff – who wouldn't trust her?

Posted at the door, I watch her spike
the marriage bed with handfuls of confetti,
discreet as fallout. Smiling, she swings back
towards me again, a natural disaster.

Bedfellows

An inch or so above the bed
   the yellow blindspot hovers
where the last incumbent's greasy head
   has worn away the flowers.

Every night I have to rest
   my head in his dead halo;
I feel his heart tick in my wrist;
   then, below the pillow,

his suffocated voice resumes
   its dreary innuendo:
there are other ways to leave the room
   than the door and the window

Countdown

These nights blink over like the clicks
that segregate the numbered frames
of a bad art movie: overlong,
shot in cheesy monochrome,
all doubletalk, obligatory sex
and no plot; the only dénouement

when the spool unravels to expose
the glare our shapes had spun across.

Beltane

(i)

Poppy, or Heaven, or Mellow slips
back into the room with two weak coffees.
She skinks a little rum into the cups,
wrestles her fat legs into a half-lotus
and relights the doup of her cigarette.

Though it does no good, every night she burns
the ragged cones of moxa on your chest.
You hardly talk: a purple rash is passed
between you, like an angry correspondence.
'There's no more water.' 'It's OK, I'll go out.'

Four months since the firestorm tore
from parish to parish, hill to sister hill.
You gallop down the unlit spiral stair:
Clatto, Lucklaw, Craigowl, Kinnoul.
The great stone blades whack past underfoot.

(ii)

Whether the cattle were driven through the blaze
to purify the strain, or purge their souls
in preparation for the sacrifice
remains unclear; though the rubbish about *Baal*
is beyond the scope of scientific debate.

Nil Nil

Just as any truly accurate representation of a particular
geography can only exist on a scale of 1:1 (imagine the
vast, rustling map of Burgundy, say, settling over it like a
freshly-starched sheet!) so it is with all our abandoned
histories, those ignoble lines of succession that end in
neither triumph nor disaster, but merely plunge on into
deeper and deeper obscurity; only in the infinite ghost-
libraries of the imagination – their only possible analo-
gue – can their ends be pursued, the dull and terrible facts
finally authenticated.

François Aussemain, *Pensées*

From the top, then, the zenith, the silent footage:
McGrandle, majestic in ankle-length shorts,
his golden hair shorn to an open book, sprinting
the length of the park for the long hoick forward,
his balletic toe-poke nearly bursting the roof
of the net; a shaky pan to the Erskine St End
where a plague of grey bonnets falls out of the clouds.
But ours is a game of two halves, and this game
the semi they went on to lose; from here
it's all down, from the First to the foot of the Second,
McGrandle, Visocchi and Spankie detaching
like bubbles to speed the descent into pitch-sharing,
pay-cuts, pawned silver, the Highland Division,
the absolute sitters ballooned over open goals,
the dismal nutmegs, the scores so obscene
no respectable journal will print them; though one day
Farquhar's spectacular bicycle-kick
will earn him a name-check in Monday's obituaries.
Besides the one setback – the spell of giant-killing
in the Cup (Lochee Violet, then Aberdeen Bon Accord,

the deadlock with Lochee Harp finally broken
by Farquhar's own-goal in the replay)
nothing inhibits the fifty-year slide
into Sunday League, big tartan flasks,
open hatchbacks parked squint behind goal-nets,
the half-time satsuma, the dog on the pitch,
then the Boy's Club, sponsored by Skelly Assurance,
then Skelly Dry Cleaners, then nobody;
stud-harrowed pitches with one-in-five inclines,
grim fathers and perverts with Old English Sheepdogs
lining the touch, moaning softly.
Now the unrefereed thirty-a-sides,
terrified fat boys with callipers minding
four jackets on infinite, notional fields;
ten years of dwindling, half-hearted kickabouts
leaves two little boys – Alastair Watt,
who answers to 'Forty', and wee Horace Madden,
so smelly the air seems to quiver above him –
playing desperate two-touch with a bald tennis ball
in the hour before lighting-up time.
Alastair cheats, and goes off with the ball
leaving wee Horace to hack up a stone
and dribble it home in the rain;
past the stopped swings, the dead shanty-town
of allotments, the black shell of Skelly Dry Cleaners
and into his cul-de-sac, where, accidentally,
he neatly back-heels it straight into the gutter
then tries to swank off like he meant it.

Unknown to him, it is all that remains
of a lone fighter-pilot, who, returning at dawn
to find Leuchars was not where he'd left it,
took time out to watch the Sidlaws unsheathed
from their great black tarpaulin, the haar burn off Tayport
and Venus melt into Carnoustie, igniting
the shoreline; no wind, not a cloud in the sky

and no one around to admire the discretion
of his unscheduled exit: the engine plopped out
and would not re-engage, sending him silently
twirling away like an ash-key,
his attempt to bail out only partly successful,
yesterday having been April the 1st –
the ripcord unleashing a flurry of socks
like a sackful of doves rendered up to the heavens
in private irenicon. He caught up with the plane
on the ground, just at the instant the tank blew
and made nothing of him, save for his fillings,
his tackets, his lucky half-crown and his gallstone,
now anchored between the steel bars of a stank
that looks to be biting the bullet on this one.

In short, this is where you get off, reader;
I'll continue alone, on foot, in the failing light,
following the trail as it steadily fades
into road-repairs, birdsong, the weather, nirvana,
the plot thinning down to a point so refined
not even the angels could dance on it. Goodbye.